SOUTHERN ITALY

2023-2024.
AMALFI COAST(TRAVEL GUIDE)

BY

LINDA GRAHAM

TABLE OF CONTENTS

INTRODUCTION

DISCOVERING THE ENCHANTMENT
OF THE AMALFI COAST

Settled along the southern edge of Italy's shocking Sorrentine Peninsula, the Amalfi Coast remains as a demonstration of nature's unrivaled creativity and human resourcefulness. This thin portion of shoreline, with its sensational bluffs diving into the purplish blue waters of the Tyrrhenian Ocean, has caught the hearts of explorers for quite a long time. Welcome to our Amalfi Coast travel guide, where we welcome you to leave on a remarkable excursion through this Mediterranean heaven.

The Amalfi Coast isn't simply an objective; it is an orchestra of encounters that will leave you charmed and propelled. Here, lively towns grip to cliffsides, memorable towns uncover the insider facts of their sea past, and perfect seashores coax sun-searchers. The fragrance of lemon forests blends with the smell of newly prepared pizza, and the reverberations of old legends fit with the giggling of local people.

In the following pages, we'll direct you through each aspect of your Amalfi Coast experience. Whether you're a fearless traveler, a heartfelt vagabond, a culinary specialist, or just looking for comfort by the ocean, this guide has something for everybody.

Go along with us as we dive into the geology and area of this captivating district, investigate the best times to visit, and uncover the insider facts of arriving. Find the social subtleties, learn fundamental Italian expressions, and go with informed decisions about your facilities. Plunge into the top attractions, unexpected, yet invaluable treasures, and the delight of wandering through noteworthy rear entryways. Investigate the climbing trails, relish the cooking, and embrace the soul of mindful travel that makes your process considerably more significant.

As we explore the winding streets, beautiful towns, and charming history of the Amalfi Coast, we welcome you to drench yourself in the wizardry of this Mediterranean gem. Whether you're arranging your most memorable visit or getting back to remember the miracle, let the Amalfi Coast guide you on an odyssey of excellence, culture, and tranquility. Thus, gather your packs, set up your faculties, and prepare to set out on an undertaking that will make a permanent imprint on your heart. The charm of the Amalfi Coast is standing by. (Have an extraordinary excursion!)

GEOGRAPHY AND LOCATION

The Amalfi Coast, an entrancing stretch of shoreline in southern Italy, is eminent for its sensational excellence, beguiling towns, and stunning perspectives on the Tyrrhenian Ocean. Settled along the southern side of the Sorrentine Landmass, this seaside district is a UNESCO World Legacy Site and a well known objective for voyagers looking for both regular magnificence and rich social encounters.

GEOGRAPHICAL HIGHLIGHTS:

1: <u>LOCATION</u>: The Amalfi Coast is located in the Campania area of Italy, on the western shore of the country. It faces the Inlet of Salerno and is lined by the Sorrentine Promontory toward the north.

2: <u>TERRAIN</u>: The shoreline is portrayed by tough precipices, steep slopes canvassed in terraced grape plantations and citrus forests, and little pebbled sea shores settled inside bays.

3: <u>MOUNTAINOUS BACKDROP</u>: The Lattari Mountains give a staggering background to the Amalfi Coast, adding to its pleasant allure. These mountains cover the towns from the more extreme northern breezes, establishing a gentle and Mediterranean environment.

KEY TOWNS AND VILLAGES

1: <u>AMALFI</u>: The namesake of the locale, Amalfi is a notable town with a striking church building and a labyrinth of thin rear entryways. It was an oceanic force to be reckoned with during the Medieval times.

2: <u>POSITANO</u>: Popular for its pastel-hued structures flowing down the precipices, Positano is quite possibly the most captured town on the coast.

3: <u>RAVELLO</u>: Roosted high in the slopes, Ravello offers all encompassing perspectives and is known for its nurseries and widespread developments.

4: <u>SORRENTO</u>: While in fact situated on the northern side of the promontory, Sorrento fills in as a door to the Amalfi Coast and flaunts staggering perspectives, lemon forests, and an energetic climate.

5: <u>PRAIANO AND MAIORI/MINORI</u>: These calmer towns give a more quiet encounter and deal simple admittance to sea shores.

ACCESS AND CONNECTIVITY:

1: <u>NAPLES</u>:

The closest significant city is Naples, situated around 25 miles (40 km) north of the Amalfi Coast. It fills in as a typical passage point for explorers, with its global air terminal and very much associated train station.

TRANSPORTATION:

The Amalfi Coast is open by street and ocean. The winding waterfront street, known as the Amalfi Drive, offers stunning perspectives yet can be tight and testing to explore. Ships and boats interface the towns and deal with a grand method for investigating the coast.

SKY BLUE /AZURE WATERS:

The Tyrrhenian Ocean's sky blue waters balance delightfully with the rich plant life and brilliant structures that stick to the precipices.

GROTTOES AND CAVES:

The shore includes a few ocean caves, including the well known Grotta Smeraldo (Emerald Cave), where the daylight makes a dazzling emerald gleam inside the cave.

FLORA AND FAUNA:

The gentle environment upholds different verdure, including lemon and olive trees. The waterfront waters are home to different marine life.

The Amalfi Coast's extraordinary topography and area make it a superb objective for explorers looking for a mix of normal marvel, social submersion, and Mediterranean unwinding. Whether you're investigating the memorable towns, climbing the rough ways, or just partaking in the perspectives from a cliffside bistro, the topography of the Amalfi Coast makes way for a remarkable encounter.

WHY VISIT THE AMALFI COAST

The Amalfi Coast, frequently alluded to as the "Heavenly Coast" (Costiera Divina), is an objective that typifies the actual pith of what puts Italy a world-on the map travel objective. This shocking waterfront locale on the southern edge of the Sorrentine Promontory is a position of unrivaled magnificence, history, and culture, drawing voyagers from around the globe.

Here are convincing justifications for why you ought to consider visiting the Amalfi Coast:

1: <u>SPLENDOR</u>:

The Amalfi Coast's rough precipices, rich slopes, and perfectly clear waters consolidate to make a scene of unrivaled magnificence. The sensational landscape is a photographic artist's fantasy and a heaven for nature lovers. Whether you're looking at the sky blue ocean from a cliff top town or climbing along old ways, the perspectives are essentially stunning.

2: <u>ENCHANTING SEASIDE TOWNS</u>:

The Amalfi Coast is speckled with beautiful towns and towns, each with its own extraordinary person.

Investigate the tight, twisting roads of Amalfi, appreciate the pastel-shaded structures of Positano, or enjoy the serenity of Ravello roosted high over the ocean. These towns offer a brief look into Italian waterfront life at its best.

3: <u>CULTURAL HERITAGE</u>:

This locale has a rich verifiable and social legacy. Amalfi, when a strong sea republic, is home to the shocking Amalfi House of prayer and an intriguing history gallery. Ravello is famous for its traditional music shows and noteworthy manors. Wherever you turn, you'll experience leftovers of a celebrated past.

4: <u>DELICIOUS CUISINE</u>:

The Amalfi Coast is a food darling's heaven. Relish the kinds of new fish, privately developed produce, and conventional dishes like "Linguine Vongole" (pasta with mollusks) and "Limoncello," a renowned lemon alcohol. Eating at coastline eateries while watching the nightfall is a remarkable encounter.

5: <u>OUTDOOR ADVENTURES</u>:

Whether you're a devoted climber or just appreciate comfortable walks, the Amalfi Coast offers a scope of open air exercises. Climb along the renowned "Way of the Divine beings" (Sentiero Dei) for all encompassing perspectives, go ocean kayaking, or investigate the district's various caverns and grottoes by boat.

6: <u>ROMANTIC GETAWAY</u>:

With its captivating view, enchanting towns, and cozy climate, the Amalfi Coast is a top decision for couples looking for a heartfelt break. It's an optimal objective for special first nights, commemorations, or essentially celebrating love.

7: <u>CULTURAL EVENTS</u>:

Consistently, the Amalfi Coast has different widespread developments, including live events, craftsmanship shows, and strict celebrations. These occasions give a one of a kind chance to submerge yourself in nearby customs and festivities.

8: <u>RELAXATION AND WELLNESS:</u>

The serene climate of the Amalfi Coast makes it an ideal spot for unwinding and restoration. Numerous inns offer spa offices, and the quieting sound of the ocean gives a characteristic feeling of serenity.

9: <u>DOOR TO HISTORY</u>:

The Amalfi Coast is likewise an entryway to a portion of Italy's most huge verifiable destinations. Require a roadtrip to the old remains of Pompeii and Herculaneum, investigate the entrancing city of Naples, or sail to the captivating island of Capri.

10: <u>NIGHTFALL SORCERY</u>:

The Amalfi Coast is famous for its dazzling dusks. Watching the sun plunge underneath the skyline while tasting a glass of neighborhood wine is a mysterious encounter that ought not be missed.

All in all, the Amalfi Coast is an objective that enraptured the faculties and offers a large number of encounters for explorers. Whether you're attracted to its regular magnificence, social lavishness, or essentially the longing to loosen up in a stunning setting, a visit to the

Amalfi Coast guarantees recollections that will endure forever. It's where the magnificence of Italy really sparkles, and it's no big surprise that it stays a fantasy objective for so many.

WHEN TO VISIT THE AMALFI COAST

The Amalfi Coast is an all year objective, each season offering a one of a kind encounter. The best chance to visit relies upon your inclinations, whether you favor warm climate for ocean side exercises, cooler temperatures for open air undertakings, or a calmer air away from the groups. Here is a breakdown of when to visit the Amalfi Coast in view of various seasons:

1. SPRING (MARCH TO MAY):

WEATHER: Spring is a magnificent chance to visit the Amalfi Coast. The weather conditions are gentle, with temperatures slowly warming as the season advances. Expect daytime temperatures going from 15°C (59°F) in Spring to 25°C (77°F) in May.

LANDSCAPE: Spring brings rich plant life, sprouting blossoms, and fragrant citrus blooms to the district, making it a phenomenal time for nature darlings and picture takers.

ADVANTAGES: Less vacationers, lower convenience rates, and wonderful climate for outside exercises like climbing and touring.

2. SUMMER (JUNE TO AUGUST):

WEATHER: Summer is the pinnacle traveler season on the Amalfi Coast, with warm and radiant climate. Normal temperatures range from 25°C (77°F) to 30°C (86°F).

BEACHES: It's the best time for sunbathing and swimming. The waterfront towns wake up with celebrations, open air shows, and an energetic air.

DRAWBACKS: Groups can be overpowering, costs are higher, and finding convenience without advance booking can be challenging. Some climbing trails might be very hot during the day.

3. AUTUMN:(SEPTEMBER TO NOVEMBER):

WEATHER: Pre-winter is one more great chance to visit. The weather conditions stay warm in September, steadily cooling in October and November. Temperatures range from 25°C (77°F) in September to 15°C (59°F) in November.

HARVEST SEASON: September and October are perfect for encountering the grape and olive gathering celebrations. You can likewise appreciate occasional cooking with new fixings.

QUIETER: As summer swarms disseminate, you can investigate the towns and attractions effortlessly and serenity.

4.   WINTER   (DECEMBER   TO FEBRUARY):

WEATHER: Winters on the Amalfi Coast are gentle, yet it tends to be crisp, particularly in the nights. Daytime temperatures range from 10°C (50°F) to 15°C (59°F).

OFF-PEAK: This is the most un-swarmed time, going with it an incredible decision for explorers looking for isolation and lower costs. You'll have the towns and attractions to yourself.

ACTIVITIES: While swimming may be excessively cold, you can in any case appreciate social encounters, neighborhood food, and investigating the calmer side of the coast. Some climbing trails are open in the cold weather months.

Conclusively, the best chance to visit the Amalfi Coast relies upon your inclinations and what you need to encounter. Spring and pre-winter are fantastic for a lovely climate, less groups, and outside exercises.

Summer is great for ocean side sweethearts and an exuberant air, however be ready at greater expenses and groups. Winter is ideal for isolation, lower costs, and social investigation, however with cooler temperatures. At last, the Amalfi Coast offers something uniquely amazing in each season, so pick the one that lines up with your movement objectives.

HOW TO GET TO THE AMALFI COAST

The Amalfi Coast, with its dazzling scenes and enchanting towns, is a fantasy objective for some explorers. To arrive at this pleasant district on the southern bank of Italy, you have a few transportation choices, contingent upon your beginning stage and inclinations. This is an aide while heading to get to the Amalfi Coast:

1. BY AIR

international airport (NAP): Naples is the nearest significant air terminal to the Amalfi Coast, settling on it the most advantageous decision for some explorers. From Naples Air terminal, you can look over different transportation techniques to arrive at the coast, like cabs, confidential exchanges, or public transportation.

ROME: Assuming you're showing up from a worldwide objective, you could likewise think about flying into Rome's Fiumicino Air terminal (FCO) or Ciampino Air terminal (CIA). From Rome, you can take a train or transport to Naples and afterward proceed to the Amalfi Coast via train, transport, or taxi.

2. VIA TRAIN:

Naples: Assuming you show up at Naples Focal Station (Napoli Centrale), you can without much of a stretch access the Amalfi Coast. Take the Circumvesuviana train from Napoli Centrale to Sorrento, where you can move to the SITA transport for the Amalfi Coast. Then again, you can arrive at Salerno via train and take a ship or transport to Amalfi or other beachfront towns.

3. BY CAR:

Driving from Naples: Leasing a vehicle in Naples or at the air terminal gives you the adaptability to investigate the Amalfi Coast at your own speed. The most widely recognized course is to take the A3 motorway (Autostrada A3) from Naples to the Amalfi Coast. Remember that the Amalfi Drive, the seaside street (SS163), is eminent for its tight and winding streets, so drive warmly.

FROM ROME: In the event that you're coming from Rome, you can lease a vehicle and drive south along the A1 motorway and afterward the A3 motorway to Naples. From Naples, follow the bearings referenced previously.

4. BY BUS:

SITA Transports: The SITA transport organization works as an organization of transports that interface Naples, Sorrento, and different towns along the Amalfi Coast. Transports are a financial plan accommodating choice, yet they can be packed during the pinnacle traveler season.

5. BY SHIP:

Ships from Naples and Salerno: You can take a ship or hydrofoil from Naples or Salerno to towns like Amalfi, Positano, and Capri. This is a beautiful and charming method for moving toward the Amalfi Coast from the ocean.

6. PRIVATE TRANSFER:

Confidential Exchanges: For a problem free and agreeable excursion, you can orchestrate a confidential exchange from Naples Air terminal, Naples Focal Station, or other close by areas straightforwardly to your picked objective on the Amalfi Coast. This choice offers comfort and customized administration.

7. HELICOPTER:

Helicopter Move: For a really one of a kind and lavish insight, a few administrators offer helicopter moves from Naples Air terminal or other close by areas to the Amalfi Coast. This is a quick and beautiful method for arriving at your location.

8. WALKING/HIKING:

Hiking: Assuming you're brave and want to investigate the Amalfi Coast by walking, you can show up by strolling along the antiquated ways and trails that interface the towns. The most popular climbing course is the "Way of the Divine Beings" (Sentiero Dei), offering dazzling perspectives en route.

Remember that the Amalfi Coast is a well known objective, particularly in the late spring months, so it's prudent to design your transportation and facilities ahead of time to guarantee a smooth and pleasant excursion to this enrapturing seaside heaven.

VISA AND ENTRY REQUIREMENTS FOR THE AMALFI COAST

Italy, including the Amalfi Coast, is important for the Schengen Region, which permits residents of specific nations to go inside the Schengen zone for the travel industry or business purposes without a visa for short stays. Notwithstanding, passage prerequisites can differ contingent upon your ethnicity and the span of your visit. Here is an outline of visa and section necessities for the Amalfi Coast:

1. SCHENGEN VISA:

Without visa Travel: In the event that you are a resident of a Schengen Region part country or a country with visa exception concurrences with the Schengen Region (e.g., the US, Canada, Australia), you can visit Italy for as long as 90 days inside a 180-day time frame without a visa for the travel industry, conferences, or family visits.

PASSPORT VALIDITY: Your visa ought to be legitimate for something like three months past your expected takeoff date from the Schengen Region.

2. VISA-REQUIRED NATIONALS:

Assuming you are a resident of a country that doesn't have a visa exception concurrence with the Schengen Region, you should apply for a Schengen Visa through the Italian international safe haven or department in your nation of origin prior to venturing out to the Amalfi Coast.

3. RESIDENCE PERMIT HOLDERS:

In the event that you hold a home license from a Schengen country, you can by and large venture out to Italy and the Amalfi Coast for short visits without a visa, however checking your particular conditions with the Italian authorities is fundamental.

4. TRAVEL INSURANCE:

Having travel protection that covers clinical costs and bringing home while venturing out to the Amalfi Coast is energetically suggested. A few nations might require evidence of movement protection upon section.

5. BORDER CONTROL:

Italy is important for the Schengen Region, and that implies there are commonly no visa controls while going between Schengen nations. Nonetheless, traditions and character looks might be conveyed incidentally.

6. LONG-TERM VISITS:

In the event that you intend to remain in Italy and the Amalfi Coast for longer than 90 days or for purposes other than the travel industry or business, you might require a public visa or home license. Make certain to check with the Italian consulate or department in your nation of origin well ahead of your outing to grasp the prerequisites for your particular circumstance.

7. CORONAVIRUS TRAVEL LIMITATIONS:

Because of the continuous Coronavirus pandemic, passage necessities, including testing and immunization prerequisites, may change much of the time. Make certain to actually look at the most recent tourism warnings, section necessities, and wellbeing guidelines from both your nation of origin and Italy before your outing.

It's significant to confirm your particular visa and passage necessities in light of your ethnicity and travel conditions prior to arranging your visit to the Amalfi

Coast. Contact the Italian international safe haven or department in your nation of origin or really take a look at the authority site of the Italian Service of International Concerns for the most exceptional data on visa and passage necessities. Consistence with these necessities will guarantee a smooth and pleasant outing to this staggering waterfront district.

CURRENCY AND MONEY MATTERS IN THE AMALFI COAST

Figuring out the cash, banking, and cash related matters is fundamental for a smooth and charming excursion to the Amalfi Coast in Italy. Here is an extensive manual for cash and cash matters in the district:

CURRENCY:

CURRENCY NAME: The authority cash of Italy is the Euro, curtailed as EUR or €.
Money Trade:

1: BANKS AND EXCHANGE OFFICES:

Banks and trade workplaces (or trade) are the most solid spots to trade cash. They are ordinarily found in towns and urban communities, including those along the Amalfi Coast.

2: <u>ATMS (BANCOMAT)</u>:

Robotized Teller Machines (ATMs) are generally accessible in the Amalfi Coast towns, making it advantageous to pull out Euros utilizing your charge or Visa. Guarantee your card has a four-digit PIN, as this is normally expected in Italy.

3<u>: CREDIT CARDS</u>

Acceptance: Significant Visas like Visa, MasterCard, and American Express are generally acknowledged in lodgings, eateries, shops, and bigger organizations. Be that as it may, a few more modest foundations might favor cash.

<u>4: CHIP AND PIN</u>: European Visa exchanges frequently require a chip and PIN for added security. Contact your bank before your outing to guarantee your card works thusly.

TRAVELERS CHECKS:

<u>USAGE</u>: Secured checks are turning out to be more uncommon, and you might find it trying to involve them in more modest towns along the Amalfi Coast. It's fitting to depend more on charge and Visas or money.

<u>ATM WITHDRAWALS</u>:
fees:While involving ATMs in Italy, know that your bank might charge unfamiliar exchange expenses and ATM withdrawal charges. Check with your bank or Visa supplier for their charge structure.

CASH TIPS:

<u>TIPPING SOCIETY</u>: Tipping is standard yet not required in Italy. In eateries, it's generally expected to leave a little tip (for the most part around 10% of the bill) for good help. In bistros, it is valued to gather together the bill. For local area experts, drivers, and other specialist organizations, tipping is likewise standard.

BUDGETING TIPS: TO MANAGE YOUR EXPENSES:

Consider feasting in nearby trattorias and pizza joints for additional reasonable dinners.

Search for food at neighborhood markets to save money on bites and cookout supplies.

Utilize public transportation or stroll to investigate the district as opposed to depending entirely on cabs or confidential exchanges

<u>BUDGETING</u>:

Typical cost for most everyday items: The Amalfi Coast is viewed as a generally costly objective in Italy. Costs for convenience, eating, and exercises can fluctuate broadly, with top traveler season by and large being more costly.

SAFETY AND SECURITY:

<u>SAFETY</u>:
 Italy, as a rule, is ok for sightseers. Nonetheless, it's wise to practice alert while conveying money and resources. Use lodging safes when accessible and try not to show huge amounts of cash openly.

<u>BANKING HOURS</u>:

Banking Hours: Banks in Italy are ordinarily open from Monday to Friday, typically from 8:30 AM to 1:30 PM, with some resuming for a couple of hours in the early evening. They are shut on ends of the week and occasions.

Being educated about cash and cash matters before your outing to the Amalfi Coast will assist you with taking full advantage of your visit while guaranteeing your monetary exchanges go without a hitch. Moreover, consider informing your bank of your itinerary items to keep away from any possible issues with your cards while abroad.

LANGUAGE AND CULTURE IN THE AMALFI COAST

The Amalfi Coast, a district of amazing normal excellence in southern Italy, isn't just known for its dazzling scenes yet in addition for its rich social legacy and the glow of its kin. Understanding the language and culture of the Amalfi Coast can upgrade your movement experience and permit you to interface all the more profoundly with the neighborhood local area.

<u>LANGUAGE</u>:

Italian is the Authority Language: Italian is the authority language spoken in the Amalfi Coast, for what it's worth all through Italy. While numerous local people in the vacationer business communicate in English and different dialects, particularly in additional famous locations like Positano and Amalfi, it's conscious and liked if you can utilize fundamental Italian expressions.

<u>DIALECTS</u>: Notwithstanding standard Italian, a few towns in the Amalfi Coast have their own lingos. For instance, the Amalfi tongue, called "Amalfitano," is as yet spoken by a few more established occupants. While excessive for explorers, finding out about these local dialects can intrigue.

<u>CULTURE</u>:

Hospitality: Individuals of the Amalfi Coast are known for their glow and accommodation. Guests are frequently greeted wholeheartedly, and it's normal for local people to start up discussions with travelers. Try not to be shocked on the off chance that you're offered a sample of hand crafted Limoncello or nearby indulgences while eating.

ART AND CRAFTSMANSHIP:

The Amalfi Coast has a long history of workmanship and craftsmanship. You'll find nearby craftsmans making ceramics, earthenware, and complicated hand-painted tiles. Amalfi and Vietri Horse are especially popular for their earthenware production.

RELIGIOUS FESTIVALS:

The Amalfi Coast has major areas of strength for a practice, and religious celebrations assume a significant part in neighborhood culture. During these celebrations, you can observe parades, marches, and firecrackers. The Dining experience of Holy person Andrew in Amalfi and the Blowout of Holy person Rocco in Positano are prominent occasions.

CUISINE:

Food is a focal part of Amalfi Coast culture. The food is Mediterranean, including new fish, neighborhood produce, and the well known Amalfi lemons. Attempt conventional dishes like "Linguine Vongole" (pasta with shellfishes) and "Sfogliatella" (a cake loaded up with ricotta). Eating is a relaxed undertaking, and Italians take as much time as is needed getting a charge out of dinners.

NEARBY ITEMS:

The Amalfi Coast is known for its development of Limoncello, a lemon alcohol produced using neighborhood lemons. You can likewise track down magnificent neighborhood wines, olive oil, and carefully assembled paper items in towns like Amalfi.

MUSIC AND DANCE:

Music and dance are essential pieces of Amalfi Coast culture. People's music, nearby dance exhibitions, and unrecorded music can frequently be appreciated at celebrations and in neighborhood settings.

CONSERVATION:

Individuals of the Amalfi Coast are profoundly associated with their current circumstance, and there is a developing emphasis on manageable travel industry and ecological preservation. Endeavors are made to safeguard the normal magnificence of the locale.

<u>DRESS CODE</u>:

While there is no severe clothing standard for guests, Italians for the most part invest wholeheartedly in their appearance. While visiting chapels or upscale eateries, it's fitting to dress unassumingly, covering shoulders and knees.

Understanding and regarding the language and culture of the Amalfi Coast can prompt more significant collaborations with local people and a more noteworthy appreciation for the customs and legacy of this shocking waterfront district. It's an amazing chance to submerge yourself in the excellence of the scene as well as of the neighborhood lifestyle.

CHOOSING THE RIGHT AMALFI COAST TOWN

The Amalfi Coast in southern Italy is well known for its shocking scenes, beguiling towns, and lively culture. Every town along this beautiful shoreline has its own special person and allure. While arranging your visit, it's critical to pick the right Amalfi Coast town that lines up with your inclinations and travel objectives. Here is a manual for assist you with settling on the ideal decision:

1. AMALFI:

CHARACTER: The town of Amalfi is the namesake of the coast and holds a rich history as a sea republic. It's a clamoring town with a beautiful harbor, bright structures, and tight roads.

ATTRACTIONS: Visit the staggering Amalfi Church (Duomo di Amalfi), investigate the noteworthy Piazza del Duomo, and partake in the neighborhood's sea shores.

ACCESSIBILITY: Amalfi is very much associated with ship and transport administrations, making it an extraordinary focal center for investigating the coast.

2. **POSITANO**:

CHARACTER: Positano is one of the most famous towns on the Amalfi Coast, known for its pastel-shaded structures flowing down steep precipices.

ATTRACTIONS: Partake in the lovely Spiaggia Grande ocean side, walk around thin rear entryways fixed with stores, and visit the Congregation of St Nick Maria Assunta.

ROMANTIC SETTING: Positano is in many cases thought to be perhaps the most heartfelt town on the coast, pursuing it as a famous decision for honeymooners and couples.

3. **RAVELLO**:

CHARACTER: Roosted high in the slopes above Amalfi and Minori, Ravello offers a tranquil and raised escape with all encompassing perspectives.

ATTRACTIONS: Investigate the wonderfully arranged nurseries of Estate Rufolo and Manor Cimbrone, go to old style music shows, and partake in the serene air.

<u>SOCIAL WEALTH</u>: Ravello is known for its far-reaching developments and has enlivened specialists and essayists for a really long time.

4. SORRENTO:

<u>CHARACTER</u>: While in fact on the northern side of the Sorrentine Landmass, Sorrento fills in as a door to the Amalfi Coast and offers shocking perspectives on Mount Vesuvius and Naples.

<u>ATTRACTIONS</u>: Investigate the memorable focus, visit the Duomo and the Shelter of San Francesco, and partake in Sorrento's vivacious environment.

<u>ACCESSIBILITY</u>: Sorrento is very much associated via train, ship, and transport administrations, making it a helpful base for investigating the district.

5. PRAIANO AND MAIORI/MINORI

<u>CHARACTER</u>: These towns offer a more peaceful encounter contrasted with the more occupied Amalfi and Positano.

<u>ATTRACTIONS</u>: Appreciate calmer sea shores, visit the places of worship, and investigate the nearby shops and eateries.

<u>RELAXATION</u>: Praiano and Maiori/Minori are great in the event that you look for a more serene climate away from the groups.

While picking the right Amalfi Coast town, consider factors, for example, your movement style, interests, and needs. Whether you're looking for lively nightlife, heartfelt excursions, social encounters, or a peaceful departure, there's a town on the Amalfi Coast that is ideally suited for you.

Every town adds to the district's general appeal, and investigating various towns during your visit can give a balanced Amalfi Coast insight.

ACCOMMODATION OPTIONS IN AMALFI COAST

The Amalfi Coast, with its shocking vistas and beguiling towns, offers a scope of convenience choices to suit different financial plans and inclinations. From lavish lodgings roosted on bluffs to comfortable family-run overnight boarding houses, here's a manual for the sorts of convenience you can track down in this lovely district:

1. LUXURY HOTELS

CHARACTER: The Amalfi Coast brags a few of the world's most rich inns, offering stunning perspectives, first class administration, and sumptuous conveniences.

LOCATION: Numerous lavish lodgings are roosted on bluffs ignoring the ocean, giving shocking scenes of the shore.

FEATURES: Expect open suites, confidential porches, limitlessness pools, connoisseur feasting, and spa offices.

Prominent Areas: Search for choices in Positano, Ravello, and Amalfi for the absolute most lavish decisions.

2. **BOUTIQUE HOTELS:**

CHARACTER: Shop inns on the Amalfi Coast join extravagance with a novel and close air.

LOCATION: They can be tracked down in different towns, frequently concealed in enchanting rear entryways or notable structures.

FEATURES: Store lodgings offer customized administration, sleek style, and a comfortable climate. Some have wonderful nurseries or roof porches.

3. **BED AND BREAKFASTS (B&BS):**

CHARACTER: Family-run B&Bs are normal along the Amalfi Coast and give a warm and valid experience.

LOCATION: You can track down B&Bs in different towns, including more modest, calmer ones.

FEATURES: Anticipate agreeable rooms, custom made morning meals, and the opportunity to connect with nearby has who can give insider tips.

4. **VACATION RENTALS:**

CHARACTER: Get-away rentals, including condos and manors, offer a usual hangout spot insight.

LOCATION: They are accessible in towns and provincial regions, ideal for the people who favor more autonomy.

FEATURES: Rentals accompany completely prepared kitchens and living spaces, making them reasonable for families or longer stays.

5. **MID-RANGE HOTELS:**

CHARACTER: Mid-range inns give a harmony among solace and reasonableness.

LOCATION: You can track them in most Amalfi Coast towns.

FEATURES: These lodgings offer agreeable rooms, frequently with ocean sees, and may incorporate conveniences like pools and on location eating.

6. **HOSTELS**:

CHARACTER: Frugal voyagers can find lodgings offering residence style facilities and confidential rooms.
LOCATION: Lodgings are more normal in towns like Amalfi and Positano.
FEATURES: Lodgings give a social environment, collective kitchens, and reasonable choices for youthful explorers.

7. **AGRITURISMI**:

CHARACTER: Agriturismi are rustic facilities frequently found in the wide open encompassing the Amalfi Coast.
LOCATION: These ranch stays offer a tranquil retreat from the seaside swarms.

<u>FEATURES</u>: Visitors can encounter neighborhood horticulture, appreciate hand crafted dinners, and enjoy the quietness of the open country.

8. **CAMPING**:

<u>CHARACTER</u>: Setting up camp aficionados can find camping areas along the Amalfi Coast, however they are restricted.

<u>LOCATION</u>: Campsites are normally found somewhat inland as opposed to right on the coast.

<u>FEATURES</u>: Fundamental offices for tents and RVs are accessible, giving a financial plan cordial choice to nature darlings.

While picking convenience in the Amalfi Coast, consider factors like your financial plan, favored area, and the kind of involvement you need. It's prudent to book well ahead of time, particularly during the pinnacle vacationer season, to get your favored housing. Despite where you stay, the Amalfi Coast's regular excellence and warm friendliness will make your excursion an essential one.

BOOKING TIPS AND RECOMMENDATIONS FOR YOUR AMALFI COAST TRIP

Booking facilities and arranging your outing to the Amalfi Coast can be a compensating experience when done well. Here are a few hints and suggestions to assist you with capitalizing on your excursion:

1. BOOK EARLY: The Amalfi Coast is an exceptionally sought-after objective, particularly during the pinnacle late spring months. To get the best facilities and get better rates, booking great ahead of time, in a perfect world a couple of months before your trip is prudent.

2. PICK THE RIGHT SEASON: Consider the season you need to visit. While summer offers warm climate and dynamic beachfront life, spring and fall are less packed, offer milder climate for open air exercises, and may give better rates on facilities.

3.FLEXIBLE TRAVEL DATES: In the event that is conceivable, be adaptable with your movement dates. Costs for facilities can change essentially contingent upon the day of the week and the season. Mid-week stays might be more reasonable than ends of the week.

**4.STAY IN MULTIPLE TOWNS:

Investigating various towns along the Amalfi Coast is essential for the appeal. Consider remaining in more than one town during your outing to encounter the extraordinary person of each. Amalfi, Positano, Ravello, and Sorrento are famous choices.

**5. TRANSPORTATION CONSIDERATIONS:

Proximity to Transport: Pick facilities near transportation center points like bus stations, ship terminals, or train stations to facilitate your movement inside the area.
Leaving: On the off chance that you're leasing a vehicle, guarantee that your convenience offers leaving, as leaving can be restricted and costly in certain towns.

6. READ REVIEWS:

Read customer feedback on reputable sites like TripAdvisor, Booking.com, and Airbnb prior to making a reservation. You can make better decisions with the help of real-life experiences and the perspectives of other guests.

**7. BOOK DIRECTLY:

While outsider booking sites are advantageous, consider booking straightforwardly with the lodging or convenience whenever the situation allows. This can some of the time bring about better rates, additional advantages, and a more customized insight.

**8.CANCELLATION POLICIES:

 Really look at the crossing out approaches of your picked facilities. In uncertain times, flexible cancellation policies can provide peace of mind.

**9.LOCAL EXPERIENCES:

Search for facilities that offer remarkable encounters, like cooking classes, wine samplings, or direct visits. These can add an exceptional touch to your visit.

**10. PACK LIGHT:

Numerous Amalfi Coast facilities are situated in memorable structures without any lifts, and roads can be limited and sloping. Pressing light will make exploring your direction to your housing a lot simpler.

11. REMAIN NEARBY:

Consider remaining in more modest, family-run facilities like overnight boarding houses (B&Bs) or store lodgings. These choices frequently give a more credible encounter and an opportunity to connect with the neighborhood.

12. LEARN SOME ITALIAN:

While numerous local people communicate in English, really trying to gain proficiency with a couple of essential Italian expressions can go far regarding social submersion and building compatibility with the occupants.

13. PREPARE AHEAD:

Past facilities, plan your exercises, visits, and café reservations ahead of time, particularly on the off chance that there are explicit places or encounters you would rather not miss.

By following these booking tips and proposals, you can guarantee a smooth and charming excursion to the Amalfi Coast, where you can drench yourself in the excellence, culture, and cordiality of this staggering beach front locale.

TOP ATTRACTIONS

The Amalfi Coast in southern Italy is an incredibly famous objective well known for its emotional shoreline, beautiful towns, and rich social legacy. Visiting the Amalfi Coast is like venturing into a postcard, with shocking normal excellence and verifiable destinations everywhere. Here are a portion of the top attractions in the Amalfi Coast that you won't have any desire to miss:

1. AMALFI TOWN:

Amalfi Cathedral (Duomo di Amalfi): A masterpiece of Arab-Norman architecture, this Romanesque cathedral was built in the 9th century. Its staggering exterior and noteworthy inside make it a must-visit.
PIAZZA DEL DUOMO:
The focal square of Amalfi is a clamoring center point of action encompassed by bistros, shops, and the famous flight of stairs prompting the church.

Museum of Paper (Museo della Carta): Find out about the exceptionally old practice of papermaking in Amalfi at this captivating exhibition hall housed in an old paper plant.

2. POSITANO:

SPIAGGIA GRANDE: The principal ocean side in Positano is a pleasant spot with vivid umbrellas, clear waters, and the town's unique pastel-hued structures as a setting.

CHURCH OF SANTA MARIA ASSUNTA: The distinctive dome of this beautiful church and the Madonna icon inside, both designed in the Byzantine style, make it famous.

PATH OF THE GODS(SENTIERO DEI): This popular climbing trail offers stunning perspectives on the shoreline and is an unquestionable requirement for nature devotees.

3. **RAVELLO**:

<u>VILLA RUFOLO</u>: Investigate the shocking nurseries of Estate Rufolo, which motivated Richard Wagner. The yearly Ravello Celebration highlights traditional music shows in this charming setting.

<u>VILLA CIMBRONE</u>: Manor Cimbrone is renowned for its "Porch of Limitlessness," offering the absolute most dazzling perspectives on the coast.

<u>RAVELLO CATHEDRAL (DUOMO DI RAVELLO)</u>: Visit the enchanting basilica in Ravello's focal square.

4. **SORRENTO**:

<u>PIAZZA TASSO</u>: Sorrento's fundamental square is an exuberant social event place encompassed by bistros and shops. It's named after the artist Torquato Tasso, brought into the world in Sorrento.

<u>MARINA GRANDE</u>: The fishing town of Marina Grande is a pleasant spot for fish eating and unwinding.

<u>LEMON ORCHARDS</u>: Sorrento is popular for its lemon forests, where you can taste Limoncello, a nearby lemon alcohol.

5. CAPRI:

GROTTA AZZURRA (BLUE GROTTO) : Take a boat visit to the Blue Cavern, an ocean cave with shocking blue waters that make a strange air.

VILLA SAN MICHELE: Visit the manor of Axel Munthe, a Swedish doctor and creator, which is currently a gallery with delightful nurseries and all encompassing perspectives.

CAPRI TOWN: Investigate the beguiling roads of Capri, loaded up with architect shops, bistros, and pleasant squares.

6. **FURORE**:

<u>FJORD OF FURORE</u>: This regular fjord, with its perfectly clear waters, is an unexpected, yet invaluable treasure along the coast and a superb spot for swimming.

<u>FURORE BRIDGE</u>: The town of Furore is known for its emotional extension, which traverses a profound chasm and gives stupendous perspectives.

These are only a couple of the top attractions you can investigate on the Amalfi Coast. Whether you're keen on history, workmanship, normal magnificence, or just partaking in the Mediterranean way of life, the Amalfi Coast brings something to the table for each explorer.

GETTING AROUND THE AMALFI COAST: A COMPLETE GUIDE

The Amalfi Coast in southern Italy is famous for its breathtaking landscapes, picturesque towns, and winding coastal roads. Investigating this locale can be an undertaking in itself, with different transportation choices accessible. Here is an exhaustive aide on getting around the Amalfi Coast:

**1. BY CAR:

VEHICLE RENTAL: Leasing a vehicle is a famous decision for explorers who need adaptability and freedom. In any case, remember that the tight and twisting streets along the Amalfi Coast can be trying to explore, particularly for those not acclimated with such territory.

PARKING: Stopping can be restricted and costly in certain towns. Search for facilities that deal with leaving assuming you intend to lease a vehicle.

**2. BY BUS:

SITA TRANSPORTS: The SITA transport organization works as a complete organization of transports interfacing the towns along the coast. This is an affordable method for voyaging, yet transports can be packed during top vacationer season.

PICTURESQUE RIDES: Transport rides along the Amalfi Coast offer the absolute most picturesque perspectives on the planet, however they can likewise be hair-raising because of the limited streets and steep precipices.

**3. BY SHIP:

SHIPS AND HYDROFOILS: Going by ship or hydrofoil is a fabulous method for partaking in the staggering beach front perspectives from the ocean. You can arrive at different towns, including Amalfi, Positano, and Capri, by water.

SHIP ADMINISTRATIONS: There are normal ship administrations from Naples, Sorrento, and Salerno to the Amalfi Coast. Really look at timetables and accessibility, particularly during the off-top season.

**4. VIA TRAIN:

TRAINS TO SORRENTO: The closest train station to the Amalfi Coast is Sorrento. You can take a train to

Sorrento from Naples, where you can then interface with other transportation choices.

CIRCUMVESUVIANA TRAIN: The Circumvesuviana train from Naples to Sorrento is an affordable option. In any case, it may very well be packed, particularly in the mid-year.

5. BY TAXI AND PRIVATE TRANSFER:

TAXIS: Taxis are accessible in many towns, and they can be recruited for little excursions or day visits. Make certain to settle on the passage prior to beginning your excursion.

PRIVATE TRANSFER: Confidential exchange administrations offer solace and comfort, particularly while going with baggage. Private transportation from train stations or airports can be arranged by many hotels.

**6. BY WALKING AND CLIMBING:

WALKING: The Amalfi Coast is home to numerous small towns that welcome pedestrians. Investigating by walking permits you to submerge yourself in the neighborhood culture.

HIKING: The Amalfi Coast offers probably the most grand climbing trails in Italy. The "Way of the Divine beings" (Sentiero Dei) and the "Valle Ferriere" are well known decisions for climbers.

7.RENTING SCOOTERS OR BICYCLES:

SCOOTERS: Leasing a bike can be an exhilarating method for investigating the coast. Be that as it may, the streets are testing, and you ought to have related knowledge.

BICYCLES: A few towns offer bike rentals, and riding along the coast can be a charming method for taking in the perspectives.

8. TIPS FOR LOCAL TRANSPORTATION:

TIMETABLES: Focus on transportation schedules, particularly for transports and ships, as they can shift via season.

TICKETS: Transport tickets can be bought at neighborhood tabacchi (tobacco shops) or on the actual transport. For ships, purchasing tickets at the port is ideal.

Getting around the Amalfi Coast can be an undertaking loaded up with amazing landscape and social encounters. Contingent upon your inclinations and travel style, you can look over a scope of transportation choices to investigate this captivating locale at your own speed.

SAFETY AND HEALTH TIPS FOR TRAVELING IN THE AMALFI COAST

The Amalfi Coast is a spellbinding location in southern Italy, famous for its normal excellence and social extravagance. Even though it's generally safe to go there, it's important to know about health and safety precautions for a safe and enjoyable trip. Here are a few hints to assist you with remaining protected and sound in the Amalfi Coast:

SAFETY TIPS:

<u>SUN SECURITY</u>: Especially in the summer, the Mediterranean sun can be intense. Wearing a hat with a wide brim, sunglasses, and sunscreen will help you stay safe. During the hottest parts of the day, drink plenty of water and look for shade.

<u>WATER SECURITY</u>: Assuming that you intend to swim, be aware of the ocean conditions. A few seashores might be serious areas of strength for have or rough regions. Continuously adhere to lifeguard guidelines and swim in assigned regions.

<u>DRIVING CAUTION</u>: In the event that you're leasing a vehicle to investigate the Amalfi Coast, practice alert on the winding and restricted streets. Be ready for difficult maneuvers and steep precipices. Drive cautiously and observe local traffic regulations.

<u>PICKPOCKET AWARENESS</u>: While the Amalfi Coast is by and large protected, pickpocketing can happen in packed vacationer regions. Keep your possessions secure, utilize hostile burglary packs, and be cautious in occupied places.

<u>RESPECT LOCAL CUSTOMS</u>: Italians are for the most part well disposed and inviting, however regarding neighborhood customs and traditions is fundamental. Dress unobtrusively while visiting houses of worship, cover your shoulders, and try not to wear swimwear in non-ocean side regions.

<u>EMERGENCY SERVICES</u>: Learn the emergency contact information in Italy: 112 for general crises, 113 for police, 118 for health related crises, and 115 for the local group of fire-fighters.

HEALTH TIPS:

<u>TRAVEL INSURANCE</u>: Having comprehensive travel insurance that covers medical costs and, in the event of an emergency, evacuation is highly recommended.

<u>PROFESSIONALLY PRESCRIBED PRESCRIPTIONS</u>: On the off chance that you require doctor prescribed meds, carry a more than adequate stockpile with you, alongside a duplicate of your medicine. Make sure the medications are still in the original containers with labels.

<u>MEDICAL CARE OFFICES</u>: Italy has an advanced medical care framework with current clinics and centers. In the event of a health related crisis, make a beeline for the closest clinic or contact the crisis administrations.

<u>WATER</u>: Faucet water in many pieces of the Amalfi Coast is protected to drink. In any case, on the off chance that you have a touchy stomach, you might lean toward filtered water.

<u>FOOD SAFETY</u>: Partake in the delectable Italian cooking, yet practice alert with road food and in little nearby restaurants. Search for places with great cleanliness rehearses, and guarantee that food is entirely cooked.

INSECT PROTECTION: In the hotter months, there can be mosquitoes. Use bug repellent and think about wearing long sleeves and jeans at night.

CORONAVIRUS CONSIDERATION: Know about any Coronavirus limitations, testing necessities, and wellbeing conventions that might be set up during your visit. Stay up with the latest with the most recent tourism warnings and necessities.

PHARMACIES: Drug stores () are normal in towns and urban communities and can give non-prescription meds, as well as guidance on minor medical problems.

VACCINATIONS FOR TRIPS: Check with your medical care supplier for any prescribed inoculations prior to making a trip to Italy.

You can have a stress-free and enjoyable trip to the Amalfi Coast if you adhere to these health and safety guidelines. Recollect that presence of mind, precautionary measures and familiarity with your environmental elements go far in guaranteeing a protected and noteworthy involvement with this lovely district.

MONEY-SAVING TIPS FOR VISITING THE AMALFI COAST

The Amalfi Coast is known for its dazzling magnificence, however it can likewise be an expensive objective. However, if you plan well and stick to your budget, you can enjoy this amazing region without spending a fortune. Here are some ways to save cash for your outing to the Amalfi Coast:

1. **VISIT DURING THE SHOULDER SEASON:**

Consider going in the shoulder times of spring (April to early June) and fall (September to October). You'll find less groups, lower convenience costs, and milder climate.

2. BOOK ACCOMMODATION AHEAD OF TIME:

Secure your facilities well ahead of time to get to better rates and stay away from somewhat late cost climbs, particularly during top mid year months.

3. CHOOSE SMALLER TOWNS:

While the significant towns like Positano and Amalfi are famous, consider remaining in more modest, less touristy towns like Praiano, Maiori, or Minori. Frequently, dining and lodging options are less expensive.

4. SELF-CATERING ACCOMMODATION:

Think about booking get-away rentals or lofts with kitchen offices. This permits you to set up a portion of your feasts, getting a good deal on eating costs.

5. LOCAL STORES:

Shop at nearby business sectors for new produce, cheeses, and different fixings. Appreciate picnics on the

ocean front or in picturesque spots, which can be both
spending plans agreeable and significant.

6. EAT WHERE LOCAL PEOPLE EAT:

Search out nearby trattorias, pizza joints, and pastry
kitchens for sensibly evaluated feasts. These foundations
frequently offer bona fide Italian cooking at additional
reasonable costs than upscale cafés.

7. WATER REFILL:

Convey a reusable water jug and top off it from public
wellsprings or request faucet water at eateries. This will
save you from purchasing filtered water over the course
of the day.

8. UTILIZE PUBLIC TRANSPORTATION:

The SITA transport framework associates the towns
along the Amalfi Coast and is an efficient method for
voyaging. Purchase a day pass for limitless rides to save
money on transportation costs.

9. AVOID THE RENTAL VEHICLE:

Except if you intend to investigate past the Amalfi Coast, you may not require a rental vehicle. In many towns, parking can be expensive and scarce, and the winding coastal roads can be difficult to navigate.

10. TRAVEL BY FOOT:

Strolling is one of the most mind-blowing ways of investigating the appeal of the Amalfi Coast's towns. By exploring on foot, you can save money on transportation because many attractions are within walking distance.

11. FREE AND MINIMAL EXPENSE EXERCISES:

Partake in the district's regular excellence by climbing on the various paths, sunbathing on open sea shores, and investigating noteworthy places of worship and squares — which are all commonly free or minimal expense.

12. VISIT FREE ATTRACTIONS:

Exploit free attractions like the beautiful towns themselves, the picturesque perspectives, and the beguiling roads loaded up with neighborhood culture.

13. **PLAN YOUR ACTIVITIES**:

- Plan your exercises ahead of time to guarantee you take advantage of your time and keep away from superfluous costs on somewhat late visits or exercises.

14. **LOCAL EXPERIENCES**:

Take part in nearby encounters like cooking classes, wine samplings, or direct visits, as these can be more reasonable and give a more profound association with the district.

15. **PAY ATTENTION TO EXCHANGE RATES:**

Keep an eye on the rates of exchange and think about changing your money at the local bank rather than at the airport or in tourist areas for better rates.

With cautious preparation and these ways to save cash, you can partake in the excellence, culture, and cooking of the Amalfi Coast without overspending, making your excursion both important and a spending plan cordial.

ESSENTIAL ITEMS TO PACK FOR YOUR TRIP TO THE AMALFI COAST

The Amalfi Coast, with its dazzling scenes and beguiling towns, is a location that joins both normal magnificence and social extravagance. To take advantage of your visit, it's fundamental to pack shrewdly. Here is a rundown of fundamental things to consider while pressing for your excursion to the Amalfi Coast:

1. TRAVEL DOCUMENTS/RECORDS:

IDENTIFICATION AND VISA:

 Check to see that your passport still has validity for at least six months after the date you planned to leave. Actually take a look at visa necessities for your identity.

TRAVEL INSURANCE: Buy exhaustive travel protection that covers health related crises, trip abrogations, and any likely accidents.

PRINTED ITINERARY/SCHEDULE: Have printed duplicates of your flight and convenience reservations, as well as any visit appointments.

DRIVER'S LICENSE/PERMIT: On the off chance that you intend to lease a vehicle, bring your driver's permit and a Global Driving Grant (IDP) whenever required.

2. CLOTHING:

COMFORTABLE STROLLING SHOES: Tough and open to strolling shoes or shoes are fundamental for investigating the towns and climbing trails.

CLOTHING THAT IS LIGHT: For warm weather, bring shorts, t-shirts, and summer dresses that are light and breathable.

SUN SECURITY: Bring a wide-overflowed cap, shades, and sunscreen to safeguard yourself from the Mediterranean sun.

SWIMWEAR: Remember your bathing suit for oceanside days or pool relaxing.

LIGHT COAT OR SWEATER: Indeed, even in summer, nights can be cooler, so bring a lightweight coat or sweater.

COMFORTABLE SHOES: An agreeable set of shoes is helpful for walking around the ocean side or partaking in a casual night.

3. ACCESSORIES FOR TRAVEL:

POWER ADAPTER: Italy utilizes European-style Type C and Type F electrical plugs, so bring the proper connectors for your electronic gadgets.

CHARGER: Keep your gadgets charged while in a hurry with a convenient charger or power bank.

TRAVEL WALLET: A movement wallet with RFID insurance can assist with keeping your cards and reports secure.

REUSABLE WATER CONTAINER: Convey a reusable water container to remain hydrated while investigating.

DAYPACK OR BEACH BAG: A beach bag is handy for days spent at the beach, while a small daypack is useful for carrying essentials on outings.

UMBRELLA OR OVERCOAT: In spite of the fact that downpour is more uncommon in summer, it's really smart to pack a minimized umbrella or overcoat for good measure.

4. TOILETRIES AND PRESCRIPTIONS:

PROFESSIONALLY PRESCRIBED PRESCRIPTIONS: If you take medications that are prescribed to you, make sure you have enough and bring copies of your prescriptions.

TOILETRIES: Pack travel-sized toiletries, including cleanser, conditioner, cleanser, and a toothbrush.

FIRST AID KITS: A fundamental emergency treatment unit with things like glue wraps, pain killers, and movement infection medicine can be helpful.

5. MISCELLANEOUS:

CAMERA AND ADORNMENTS: Catch the shocking landscape with a camera or cell phone and remember memory cards, chargers, and additional batteries.

GUIDE TO LANGUAGES: A phrasebook or language guide can be convenient for speaking with local people.

TRAVEL LOCKS: Use TSA-supported makemytrip locks to get your gear and resources.

TRAVEL PILLOW AND EYE MASK: Remain open during long excursions with a movement pad and eye veil.

<u>TRAVEL ADAPTERS</u>: Carry head out connectors to charge your electronic gadgets.

6. MONEY AND CARDS:

<u>ATM/DEBIT/CREDIT CARDS</u>: Bring a blend of installment choices. Tell your bank of your itinerary items to stay away from card issues abroad.

<u>CASH</u>: Keep some Euro cash on hand in case of an emergency, transportation, or small purchases.

7. MANUALS AND GUIDES:

<u>GUIDES AND MANUALS</u>: Physical or computerized guides and manuals can be priceless for exploring the region and finding nearby attractions.
You will be well-prepared for your trip to the Amalfi Coast and ready to make the most of your adventure in this captivating region if you pack these essential items.

ITINERARIES AND DAY TRIPS FOR EXPLORING THE AMALFI COAST

The Amalfi Coast has a lot to offer in terms of beauty, culture, and history. You can spend a few days there or take day trips from nearby cities to see it all. Here are a few schedule thoughts and road trip choices to assist you with capitalizing on your visit to this shocking district of Italy:

1. CLASSIC AMALFI COAST ITINERARY (3-5 Days):

DAY 1: AMALFI TOWN

Show up in Naples and move to the Amalfi Coast.
Go through your most memorable night investigating Amalfi Town, visiting the house of God, and partaking in a customary Italian supper.

DAY 2: POSITANO

Requires a road trip to Positano, known for its beautiful precipices and dynamic roads.
Investigate the town, unwind on the Spiaggia Grande ocean side, and visit the Congregation of St Nick Maria Assunta.

DAY 3: RAVELLO

Make a beeline for Ravello, known for its dazzling nurseries at Manor Rufolo and Estate Cimbrone.
Go to an old style music show or partake in the town's social contributions.

DAY 4: SORRENTO

Go to Sorrento for a road trip, investigating the memorable focus and getting a charge out of perspectives on Mount Vesuvius.
Visit the Shelter of San Francesco and attempt the nearby Limoncello alcohol.

<u>DAY 5: CAPRI</u>

Take a ship to the island of Capri for a day of investigating.
Visit the Blue Cavern, Anacapri, and the beguiling roads of Capri Town prior to getting back to the Amalfi Coast.

2. EXTENDED AMALFI COAST EXPLORATION (7-10 DAYS):

<u>DAY 1-3:</u> Sorrento and the Peninsula Make the most of your first few days in Sorrento by exploring the city and taking day trips to your preferred Amalfi Coast towns.

DAY 4-6: Towns on the Amalfi Coast Staying in towns like Amalfi, Positano, and Ravello on the Amalfi Coast lets you fully experience each place.

DAY 7-10: Naples and the Areas Nearby

Make a beeline for Naples for a couple of days and investigate the city's notable place, archeological locales like Pompeii and Herculaneum, and appreciate Neapolitan pizza.

Make sure to check neighborhood transportation timetables and book facilities ahead of time, particularly during top vacationer seasons, to capitalize on your Amalfi Coast experience. Whether you decide to investigate the district north for a few days or pick roadtrips, the Amalfi Coast offers a large number of encounters for voyagers to appreciate.

ONE-WEEK ITINERARY FOR EXPLORING THE AMALFI COAST

Seven days on the Amalfi Coast permits you to submerge yourself in the district's amazing magnificence, rich culture, and heavenly food. Here is a complete one-week schedule to capitalize on your time in this
dazzling piece of Italy:

DAY 1: ARRIVAL IN NAPLES

Show up at Naples Worldwide Air terminal (Rest) and move to your picked Amalfi Coast town (Amalfi, Positano, or Ravello).
Look into your convenience and get comfortable.
At night, investigate your town's enchanting roads, feast at a nearby eatery, and partake in your most memorable taste of Italian cooking.

DAY 2: AMALFI TOWN

Start your investigation of the Amalfi Coast with a visit to Amalfi Town.
Investigate the Amalfi House of prayer (Duomo di Amalfi) and its staggering inside.
Walk around the pleasant Piazza del Duomo and partake in a comfortable lunch at a nearby trattoria.

Go through the evening on the Spiaggia Grande ocean side or investigate the town's interesting shops.

Enjoy fresh seafood at a waterfront restaurant in the evening.

DAY 3: POSITANO TRAVEL TO POSITANO:
It is an iconic town, by morning bus or ferry.

Meander through the vivid roads, visit the Congregation of St Nick Maria Assunta, and unwind on Spiaggia Grande.

Partake in a comfortable lunch at a cliffside eatery with all encompassing perspectives.

Go through the early evening time looking for pottery and neighborhood makes.

Get back to your base town at night for supper.

DAY 4: RAVELLO

Withdraw for Ravello, a beguiling ridge town known for its nurseries and live performances.
Take a look at the stunning gardens of Villa Cimbrone and Villa Rufolo.
Go to a traditional music show or essentially relish the serene feel.
Get back to your town for the evening.

DAY 5: CAPRI

Take a ship from your town to the charming island of Capri.
Capri Town's charming streets, the Gardens of Augustus, and high-end boutiques are all worth a visit.
Take a boat visit to the Blue Cavern and other grand spots.
Get back to the Amalfi Coast at night and eat in your town.

DAY 6: SORRENTO

Go to Sorrento for a road trip and investigate the memorable focus.
Visit the House of San Francesco and the Sorrento Church.
Try Limoncello, a local lemon liqueur, for lunch at a traditional pizzeria.
In the early evening, loosen up on the seashores of Marina Grande or go for a stroll along the bluffs.
Get back to your town at night.

Day 7: Relaxation and Culinary Delights

Go through your keep going the entire day on the Amalfi Coast partaking in your number one exercises. Whether it's climbing, sunbathing on the oceanfront, or taking a cooking class, capitalize on your time.
At night, enjoy a goodbye supper at an eminent neighborhood eatery, relishing the kinds of the district.

Day 8: departure

Leave your convenience and move to Naples Global Air terminal for your takeoff flight.
This one-week schedule gives a balanced encounter of the Amalfi Coast, permitting you to investigate its most

notorious towns, relish delectable cooking, and absorb the Mediterranean feeling. To ensure a smooth and memorable trip, make sure to book your lodging and transportation in advance.

RESPONSIBLE TRAVEL PRACTICES:
MAKING A POSITIVE IMPACT ON YOUR JOURNEY:

Mindful travel, frequently alluded to as practical or eco-accommodating the travel industry, is an approach to investigating the world that focuses on the prosperity of the climate, nearby networks, and social legacy. When you travel responsibly, you not only enhance your own experiences but also make a positive contribution to the destinations you visit. Here are a few vital standards and practices to keep:

**1. REDUCE YOUR CARBON FOOTPRINT:

CHOOSE SUSTAINABLE TRANSPORTATION:

Choose eco-accommodating methods of transport, like trains, transports, and carpooling, whenever the situation allows. Consider flying less and utilizing choices like fast trains.

LIMIT DRIVING:

In the event that you lease a vehicle, pick an eco-friendly vehicle, and carpool while going with others. Reduce your speed to save gas.

BALANCE YOUR FOSSIL FUEL BYPRODUCTS:

Consider buying carbon balances to make up for the discharges produced during your excursion.

2. SUPPORT LOCAL COMMUNITIES:

PICK PRIVATELY POSSESSED FACILITIES:

Remain in privately claimed lodgings, guesthouses, or homestays to help the local area straightforwardly. Stay away from huge worldwide inn networks.

BUY LOCAL:

Shop at neighborhood markets and back craftsmans by buying high quality artworks and items. Add to the neighborhood economy by eating at privately possessed cafés.

Find out About Nearby Traditions: Regard neighborhood customs, customs, and clothing standards. Try to become familiar with a couple of essential expressions in the neighborhood language to work with correspondence.

3. PROTECT THE ENVIRONMENT :

LEAVE NO TRACE:

Follow the "Leave No Follow" standards by taking your rubbish with you, remaining on assigned trails, and not upsetting natural life or biological systems.

RETAIN RESOURCES:

Be aware of water and energy use. In your lodging, reuse towels and bedding, and turn off lights and appliances when not in use.

CONTRIBUTE TO ECO-FRIENDLY TOURS:

Choose tour operators and activities that place a strong emphasis on environmental preservation and responsible interactions with wildlife.

4. REDUCE SINGLE-USE OF PLASTICS:

BRING REUSABLE THINGS: Convey a reusable water bottle, shopping sack, and utensils to diminish plastic waste.

SAY NO TO PLASTIC STRAWS: Decline single-utilize plastic straws and select options like metal or bamboo.

CORRECTLY GET RID OF WASTE: Utilize assigned reusing and garbage removal offices when accessible.

5. PRACTICE ETHICAL WILDLIFE TOURISM:

RESEARCH ANIMAL COMMUNICATIONS:

Stay away from exercises that include hostage or abused creatures. Pick moral natural life visits that focus on creature government assistance and protection.

<u>OBSERVE WILDLIFE RESPONSIBLY</u>:

On the off chance that you experience untamed life in regular settings, maintain a protected separation and try not to take care of or upset them.

6. REDUCE WATER CONSUMPTION:

<u>SHORTEN SHOWERS</u>:

Limit your time in the shower and lessen water use in bone-dry areas.

<u>USE WATER CAREFULLY:</u>

When you are not actively using water, turn off the faucet when brushing your teeth or doing the dishes.

7. INSTRUCT/ EDUCATE YOURSELF:

<u>CULTURAL SENSITIVITY:</u> Research and find out about the neighborhood culture, history, and customs of the spots you visit. This improves your movement experience and recognizes neighborhood customs.

<u>ENVIRONMENTAL EDUCATION</u>: Instruct yourself about the ecological difficulties confronting the objective and do whatever it takes to limit your effect.

**8.ADVOCATE FOR RESPONSIBLE TRAVEL:

SPREAD MINDFULNESS:

Share your mindful travel encounters and information with others, empowering them to settle on dependable decisions.

ASSISTANCE ORGANIZATIONS:

 Add to or volunteer with associations that advance practical the travel industry and protection endeavors.

By practicing responsible travel, you can appreciate staggering experiences while leaving a positive effect on the objections you investigate. Keep in mind that preserving the world's cultural and natural treasures for future generations requires even the smallest of actions.

LOCAL CUSTOMS AND ETIQUETTE: NAVIGATING CULTURAL SENSITIVITIES ABROAD

While heading out to another objective, understanding and regarding nearby traditions and manners is crucial for cultivating positive collaborations and guaranteeing a noteworthy and deferential experience. Here are a few basic principles to remember as you explore social responsive qualities in various regions of the planet:

**1. RESEARCH BEFORE YOU GO:

Research the social norms, traditions, and customs of the place you'll be visiting prior to your trip. Understanding the neighborhood culture will assist you with keeping away from accidental social tactless acts.

2. DRESS APPROPRIATELY:

Dress unassumingly while visiting strict or moderate regions. Covering one's knees and shoulders is a sign of respect in many cultures.
Continuously take off your shoes prior to entering somebody's home, a sanctuary, or a mosque in numerous Asian and Center Eastern nations.

3. WELCOME RESPECTFULLY:

Gain proficiency with the proper method for hello individuals in the nearby language. A basic "hi" or "much obliged" in the nearby tongue can go quite far in showing regard.
In certain societies, it's standard to bow, offer a handshake, or give a slight gesture as a hello. Find out what the locals do best in the area you're visiting.

4. USE POLITE LANGUAGE:

Be aware of your language, tone, and volume while talking with local people. Do not speak loudly or use profane language.

Learn normal considerate expressions like "if it's not too much trouble, "thank you," and "excuse me" in the nearby language.

5. EATING ETIQUETTE:

Get familiar with the traditions of dining. In certain societies, it's pleasant to trust that the host will begin the feast, while in others, it's standard to start eating when the food is served.

Figure out how to utilize chopsticks or different utensils in the event that you'll feast in a district with various eating devices.

6. RESPECT RELIGIOUS PRACTICES:

While visiting strict destinations, follow the clothing regulation and act deferentially. This could mean not taking photos, covering your head, or taking off your shoes.

Keep away from public showcases of fondness close to strict destinations, as they can be viewed as insolent.

7. GIVING GIFTS:

Assuming that you intend to give gifts to local people, research fitting things and customs. A few societies have explicit customs around gift-giving.
Continuously present gifts with two hands, and never give liquor in Islamic nations except if you're certain it's OK.

8. NON-VERBAL COMMUNICATION:

Know that signals can have various implications in different societies. For instance, a thumbs-up signal is positive in certain spots however hostile in others.
Keep your feet on the ground while sitting, as showing the bottoms of your shoes can be viewed as impolite in certain societies.

9. RESPECT PERSONAL SPACE:

Keep your personal space in mind, especially in crowded places. What might be agreeable nearness for discussion in one culture might vary in another.

10. **PHOTOGRAPHY ETIQUETTE:

Continuously request authorization prior to taking photographs of people, particularly in countries or distant regions.
Regard any standards or rules with respect to photography at social or strict destinations.

11. **HAGGLING AND BARGAINING:

In certain societies, wheeling and dealing is a typical practice in business sectors. Be that as it may, it's critical to do so consciously and without animosity.

12. BE OPEN AND INQUISITIVE:

Show an interest in the nearby culture and customs. Local people appreciate when voyagers are available to learn and embrace new encounters.

Recollect that really trying to comprehend and regard neighborhood customs and behavior improves your movement experience as well as encourages positive collaborations with individuals you meet en route.

It's OK to commit errors, however exhibiting a real interest in the neighborhood culture and an eagerness to adjust will go far in making significant associations and essential encounters while voyaging.

USEFUL PHRASES IN ITALIAN FOR TRAVELERS

Italian is a wonderful language spoken in Italy as well as in different regions of the planet. Learning a couple of key expressions can extraordinarily upgrade your movement experience in Italy. The following are some travel-friendly Italian phrases:

****1. GREETINGS:

Hello: Ciao (pronounced chow)

Good morning: Buongiorno (bwohn-johr-noh)

Good afternoon: Buon pomeriggio (bwohn poh-meh-ree-djoh)

Good evening/night: Buonasera (bwoh-nah-seh-rah)

Goodbye: Arrivederci (ah-ree-veh-dehr-chee)

See you later: A più tardi (ah pyoo hard-ee)

**2. COMMON COURTESIES:

Please: Per favore (pehr fah-voh-reh)

Thank you: Grazie (grah-tsyeh)

You're welcome: Prego (preh-goh)

Excuse me/sorry: Mi scusi (mee koo-zee)

3. BASIC CONVERSATIONAL PHRASES:

Yes: Sì (see)

No: No (noh)

I don't understand: Non capisco (non kah-pee-skoh)

I don't speak Italian: Non parlo italiano (non pahr-loh ee-tah-lee-ah-noh)

What's your name?: Come ti ? (koh-meh tee kee-ah-mee?)

My name is [Your Name]: Mi [Your Name] (mee kee-ah-moh [Your Name])

How are you?: Come ? (koh-mai ?)

I'm good: Sto bene (stoh beh-neh)

I'm sorry: Mi (mee dees-pyah-cheh)

4. ASKING FOR HELP:

Can you help me?: Puoi aiutarmi? (pway ah-yoo-tahr-mee?)

Where is...?: Dov'è...? (doh-veh...?)

How much is this?: Costa ? (kwahn-toh kohs-tah kwehs-toh?)

I need a doctor: Ho bisogno di un dottore (oh bee-zoh-nyoh dee oon doht-toh-reh)

5. ORDERING FOOD AND DRINKS:

I'd like...: Vorrei... (vohr-ray...)

Water: Acqua (ah-kwah)

Wine: Vino (vee-noh)

Coffee: Caffè (kahf-feh)

The Bill, Please: Il conto, per favore (eel kohn-toh, pehr fah-voh-reh)

6. DIRECTIONS:

Where is the bathroom?: Dov'è il bagno? (doh-veh eel bahn-yoh?)

LEFT: Sinistra (see-nee-strah)

RIGHT: Destra (dehs-trah)

STRAIGHT AHEAD: Sempre (sehm-preh dree-toh)

STREET: Via (vee-ah)

BUS STOP: Fermata dell'autobus (fehr-mah-tah dehl-lah-oo-toh-boos)

7. EMERGENCIES:

HELP!: Aiuto! (ah-yoo-toh!)

FIRE: Incendio (een-chen-dyo)

POLICE: Polizia (poh-lee-ts-yah)

HOSPITAL: Ospedale (oh-speh-dah-leh).

I Need A Pharmacy: Ho bisogno di una farmacia (oh bee-zoh-nyoh dee oo-nah fahr-mah-kyah)

Learning these basic Italian phrases will not only help you navigate your way around Italy but also show respect for the local culture. Italians appreciate when travelers make an effort to speak their language, even if it's just a few words. ! (Have a great trip!)

CONCLUSION:

EXPLORING THE ENCHANTING AMALFI COAST

In closing this Amalfi Coast travel guide, we welcome you to set out on an excursion loaded up with regular excellence, rich culture, and extraordinary encounters. With its dramatic cliffs, picturesque villages, and azure waters, the Amalfi Coast is a destination that captivates every traveler.

The Amalfi Coast has a plethora of memorable sights and experiences, including the historic town of Amalfi, the vibrant cliffs of Positano, and the tranquil gardens of Ravello. Fresh seafood, freshly made pasta, and the zesty flavor of limoncello that is made locally all make up the cuisine, which is a symphony of flavors.

As you investigate this stunning district, make sure to be a dependable explorer, regarding the climate, neighborhood customs, and social legacy. Draw in with the networks you visit, support nearby organizations, and relish the genuineness of this seaside diamond.

The Amalfi Coast has something for everyone, whether you want to relax on secluded beaches, learn about ancient history at Pompeii and Herculaneum, or hike the famous Path of the Gods. It is a destination that awakens the adventurer in all of us and gives us a glimpse of the magic of the Mediterranean. It also excites the senses.

Therefore, pack your belongings, pick up a few Italian phrases, and get ready for an unforgettable journey along the winding roads and picturesque views of the Amalfi Coast. The Amalfi Coast beckons with open arms, ready to share its beauty and charm with those who dare to explore its shores, whether you're looking for romance, adventure, or relaxation. Good travels! Have an incredible outing!)